AF081593

BRICKDICTION

BRICKDICTION

A Seven Step Recovery Guide
for People Addicted to LEGO®

Bill Deen

Brickdiction: A Seven Step Recovery Guide for People Addicted to LEGO®.

Category: Humor, Hobby, Toy, Family, Children

This book has not been approved, affiliated with, licensed, or sponsored by The LEGO Group.

"LEGO" and "MINIFIGURE" are trademarks of the LEGO Group.

Product and company names mentioned herein may be the trademarks of their respective owners. Rather than use a trademark symbol with every occurrence of a trademarked name, we sometimes use the names only in an editorial fashion and to the benefit of the trademark owner, with no intention of infringement of the trademark.

Copyright © 2012 J. B. McConkie.

All rights reserved.

ISBN-10: 1468083996
ISBN-13: 978-1468083996

*Dedicated to the wives
who let us live our LEGO lives.*

(I realize there are many female AFOLs. But as a male, it was easier — and safer — for me to write this to a male reader. I mean no offense.)

*This book, and its
hope-filled message,
is presented to you
by*

"Men are men, but they were not all cast in the same mold. Bricks are bricks, and they can all be built in the same wall, but every man must be himself, walk and work as he likes, and not expect to be built into any wall to serve exactly as the man next to him."

John Wanamaker

DESCRIPTION

You know the scene. You walk into any toy store, "for the kids" (*wink wink*), to purchase just ONE toy. You come out with just about every LEGO® set the store has—for yourself. Next, you're wondering how you're going to pay the bills, and whether you'll be able to give your kids Christmas presents this year.

Brickdiction: A Seven Step Recovery Guide for People Addicted to LEGO® lays out the principles and procedures YOU can apply to YOUR life to recover from your plastic brick addiction.

Countless people have turned their lives around by going through the steps outlined in this book. You too can recover from your LEGO® addiction by working through these steps.

Recovery will be hard, but it is possible. Have hope.*

*Disclaimer: This might be a good time to point out that this whole book is a joke. (You didn't think I was actually serious, did you?)

CONTENTS

Words to Build On	p. 2
The Steps	p. 5
Introduction	p. 6
STEP ONE: Admission	p. 9
STEP TWO: Hope	p. 13
STEP THREE: Decision	p. 17
STEP FOUR: Inventory	p. 21
STEP FIVE: Admission (again!)	p. 27
STEP SIX: Amends	p. 31
STEP SEVEN: Share	p. 37
Continue the Journey	p. 41
Confession	p. 45

WORDS TO BUILD ON

LEGO – The best, greatest, most awesome (and sometimes addictive) toy in the world!

Set — A LEGO kit. An official group of bricks, sold together, with instructions showing what can be made.

LUG — LEGO Users Group. A physical or virtual group of LEGO enthusiasts (kind of like a club).

AFOL – Adult Fan of LEGO. Variations include CFOL (children) and TFOL (teens).

Brickdiction – The LEGO addiction suffered mainly by AFOLs. When someone has this they are "brickdicted."

MOC — My Own Creation. A LEGO model created without instructions, designed by the builder.

UCS — Ultimate Collectors Series. UCS sets are massive, expensive, and have almost no playability (but they look awesome!). Because of their sheer physical massiveness and financial investment, they appeal mainly to adults and other more experienced builders.

Minifig — Short for "Minifigure." These are the small, lovable, plastic people that accompany LEGO bricks.

Swooshable — A model that is easily zoomed around in a builder's hands. If a creation is swooshable, then it is easy for a builder to imagine it flying around the room. This is generally accompanied with laser, engine, or other "vroooom!" or "pew!" sounds made by the "pilot."

Example of a "swooshable" ship (a modified version of LEGO set 7965 Millenium Falcon). A smaller navigation dish, larger front, and modified gun turret make it one of my favorite MOCs. More shots at www.brickdiction.com.

THE SEVEN STEPS TO RECOVERY

1. Admit to yourself that you are powerless over bricks — that your brick life has become unmanageable.

2. Come to believe that recovery is possible, but only with the help of others.

3. Make a decision to change.

4. Make a searching and fearless plastic inventory of yourself.

5. Admit your problem to someone other than yourself. (Minifigs don't count.)

6. Make amends.

7. Share the message with others.

INTRODUCTION

First, let me start by apologizing. I'm sorry I couldn't make this book more swooshable. There's only so much a publisher can do—adding wings, wheels, and a jet engine to a book aren't possible. I also can't really make it any more aerodynamic.

Second, let me tell you just why I wrote this recovery guide.

I see a real problem in the universe. I see despair, and pain, and sorrow. But that's not what this book is about.

Besides all that, I see an overload of plastic brick fanatics. There's no inherent problem with this, except that many of these nerds—geeks, if you will—are addicted to these little plastic bricks.

That's why I wrote this book.

I hope that by writing this, I can help any addicted brick enthusiasts recover from their brick addiction (or brickdiction).

If just one life can be turned around, writing this has been worth it. May you be hopeful as you begin this journey to complete recovery.

Sincerely,

Bill Deen

P.S. On a serious note, this book *is not* meant to mock addiction recovery programs or those involved in those programs. It *is* meant to mock CFOLs, TFOLs and AFOLs like me.

STEP 1

STEP 1

STEP 1 - ADMIT YOU ARE POWERLESS OVER BRICKS

The first step in recovering from your brickdiction is to admit that you are powerless over bricks. In other words, you have to realize that your brick life has become unmanageable.

By purchasing this book, you have already acknowledged your brickdiction, at least to some extent. If instead of buying it you were gifted this book, then…wow, your problem is bigger than I thought.

If you don't complete this first step, then any other efforts your make to recover will be meaningless. So do it. Now. Don't even read further, until you've formally and officially stated that you have lost the ability to resist. Only then can you continue the process.

You do not have the emotional, physical, or mental capacity to overcome this challenge in your life by yourself. Why is this important?

In order to recover, you are going to need to have the support of others. Others often know you better than you know yourself.

STEP 2

STEP 2 - COME TO BELIEVE THAT RECOVERY IS POSSIBLE, BUT ONLY WITH THE HELP OF OTHERS

Once you have admitted that you are powerless over bricks, the next step is to recruit the people in your life who can help you become de-bricked.

You should rely on your family and friends for support. They provide the warmth, love, and understanding you need to stay away from your bricks. If members of your family are brickdicted, then they can still help. You can help each other.

If you're a member of a LUG, stay away from it. Stop going, or being involved in any way with the group. Also refrain from talking with the people you know in your LUG. Whether they do it intentionally or not, they will tempt you. Beware! The worst thing you can do when trying to recover is talk to another brick-obsessed toy geek.

You must go through a few other steps before you attempt to recruit others to your aid. So for now, just put this in the back of your mind. Later, in step 5, you'll do the first step in asking others to help. For now, just know that you CAN change. It is possible.

Have hope.

Believe!

STEP 3

STEP 3 - MAKE A DECISION TO CHANGE

This, like most of the other steps, is critical to your recovery. You MUST make a decision to change. You must be determined to live by this decision as well.

It will be much easier for you to recover if you aren't trying to decide in the moment whether you should (a) purchase another few battle packs (*They're on sale!*), or (b) stop this reckless behavior. Because you have already made your decision, you will be able to better resist your inner builder.

Start this process by reminding yourself of the reasons why you are making this decision. This will help your decision be a firmer one. By thinking through why you are making this decision, you will be better prepared to resist any temptations that may arise.

Here are some reasons other brickdicted individuals have made this decision:

- They realized they had no life outside of building.
- They physically could not fit any more bricks in their home.
- Their credit card wasn't accepted when they last attempted to purchase more bricks (*You'd think the bank would trust me!*).
- They realized that at some point they would like to retire, and their current habits would not allow that.
- They (or their loved ones) found it disturbing that the UPS guy made multiple deliveries on the same day.
- Food.
- Rent.
- Their wife decided for them.

There is an old saying, "Indecision becomes decision with time." It is important for you to make a firm, unwavering decision to turn your life around and improve yourself. By not deciding, you have decided. So watch it.

Decide now to change.

STEP 4

STEP 4 - MAKE A SEARCHING AND FEARLESS PLASTIC INVENTORY OF YOURSELF

This step will take some time. You will need to put considerable thought into this exercise, as this will be the beginning of the new and improved you.

The first step in this process is to answer, to the best of your ability, these three questions:

1. *How does my brickdiction affect me?*

2. *How does my brickdiction affect others?*

3. *What flaws in my character lead me to succumb to my brickdiction?*

Let's explore these questions individually.

How does my addiction affect me?

What are the consequences of my brickdiction? They could be financial, emotional, or physical.

You may have no social life, or your social life may consist only of interacting with other adult geeks who share your plastic passion. Or perhaps minifigs are the only "people" that you associate with.

How does my brickdiction affect others?

Don't fall into the trap of thinking about the "good" aspects of your plastic life. You may believe that building makes you more creative. You may also think that your children are blessed when you build with them. Don't allow such thoughts in your mind. They will only fuel your addiction.

Instead, think of the many negative repercussions of your hobby. If you're married, most likely your spouse is aware of your brickdiction. She may remind you that you haven't paid the last few bills, or that there's no room left on your dining room table (*"Remember, dear? That set you bought last week...?"*). She may also insist that someday you're going to want to retire, and you'll probably want to have some money when you do.

One recovering AFOL's wife went so far as to ban all visits to toy stores. She would even inspect any boxes that came in the mail, to make sure there were no plastic bricks inside.

Like most things your wife says, these words should be heard and heeded. This will greatly assist you in your recovery.

What flaws in my character lead me to succumb to my brickdiction?

This will be emotional. Are you easily angered? Do you have a poor self-image? Do you have fear, or worry about something? Are you afraid of dogs? Is there a second identity you are trying to bring out when building?

These are all thoughtful questions. At first, you'll almost assuredly deny any sort of emotional disturbances you might have. But you must consider WHY you do what you do. Are you trying to be a child again? Don't you realize you're an adult? Actually, if you are reading this, you probably don't. So never mind.

Bottom line—you need to think about what leads you to buy a complete box of 60 collectible minifigs, or what leads you to purchase seven duplicates of the *same set*. Why do you always go to the toy area of your local, big box store, even when you only have a minute to spare?

You must be completely honest with yourself. It will be difficult to answer these questions, but it's imperative to your recovery that you do. Once you understand where you are now, you can determine what you need to do to get where you want to go—to change.

There's just one more step you need to do before you begin to turn your life around.

STEP 5

STEP 5 – ADMIT YOUR PROBLEM TO SOMEONE ELSE

You must admit to someone other than yourself that you are brickdicted. (Minifigs don't count.) This will be much easier than you think, because there's almost no possible way someone in your life hasn't already noticed your situation.

If you're married, most likely it's your wife. She of course knows, but you should still admit it officially, and declare that you're attempting to recover.

You could also go to your local toy store and tell the employees there, or even the store manager. Go to customer service and ask to speak to the store manager. Ask if you can have a few minutes of their time, to make a confession.

Assuming they don't call the police (or a psychiatrist) he or she should be willing to listen to your story. (If the toy department manager calls you by your first name, then your brickdiction has gone too far, and your recovery is hopeless.)

Regardless of who you tell, all you need to do is tell them your story, and announce that you're going to improve. Tell them about your first set, and how you came out of your dark ages. Tell them about how you plan to end this vicious cycle.

Only after you have admitted your brickdiction, can you begin to turn your life around.

STEP 6

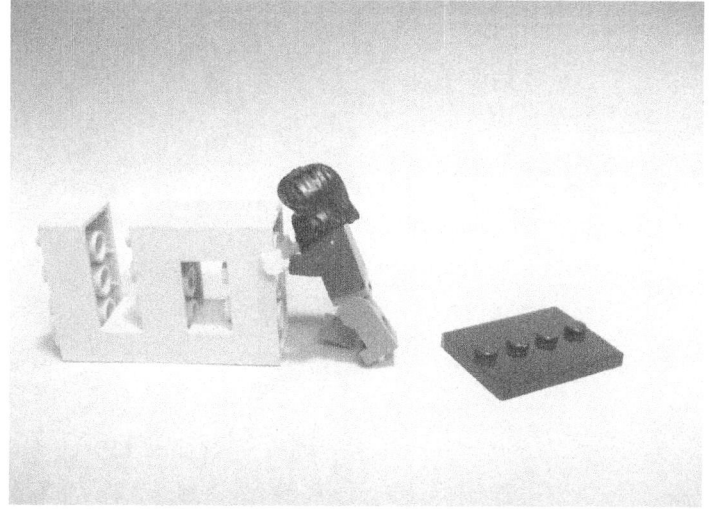

STEP 6 – MAKE AMENDS

Good job! If you've come this far, I'd like to congratulate you on your success! Pat yourself on your back. You should reward yourself by ~~going out and buying another set~~ staying home and thinking about how far you have come.

Upon completing step six, you will really begin to change your life. You cannot move forward until you have corrected, at least to some extent, your past. So if you haven't completed steps one through five, go back and do them.

This step, like building a UCS set, requires great concentration and skill. (Sorry, there is no black collector's card included with *this* book.)

Think of all of the people who have been affected by your brickdiction. You did this in step four, but this is a little different.

While thinking of these people (including yourself), think about how you could make amends to those you have negatively affected. Then, set out to do just that. It may take a while, but it's critical for your mental health that you do. Besides, it's why you bought this book!

Declutter

Chances are your bricks take up a good portion of your house. In fact, this is one of the first signs of brickdiction—when someone has a whole room devoted strictly to their MOCs. This is even more of a red flag if you spend hour upon hour in this room, have meals brought in, and/or lock it so that your kids won't see or destroy the manifestations of your creative endeavors.

Of course, there are two ways to solve this problem. You can either make more room by clearing stuff out, or make more room by making more rooms!

You could clear all of your bricks out, sell it as one big lot, and then renovate that room with the money. Or you could just add a wing to your house, and have an even bigger MOC display gallery (although this probably isn't a good idea if you're actually serious about recovering).

Hot Bricks

If you have taken bricks from anyone, return them and apologize. If you can't return them, then do your best to compensate the victim. (Note: Just because the bricks are currently part of a MOC you recently completed, that's no excuse to deprive your son, or nephew, or your neighbor's kid of bricks that rightly belong to them.)

Thank you Card

This isn't so much about making amends, but it does involve your friends and family. If you were given this book, then something you could do as part of your recovery is to send a thank you card or letter expressing your appreciation to whoever gave it to you.

All of these are ways you can make amends to yourself, and others you have harmed.

STEP 7

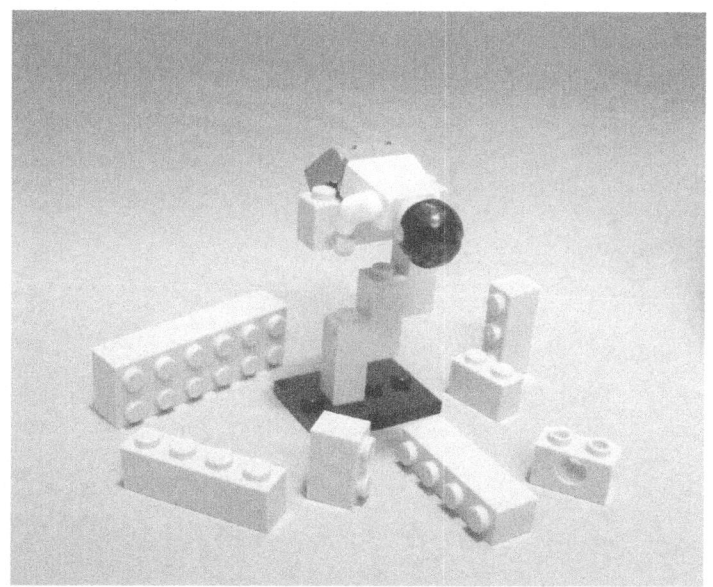

STEP 7 - SHARE THE MESSAGE WITH OTHERS

After you've made your recovery, you should try to spread this message of hope to all the brickdicted individuals you know.

As the author, I ask you—no, I plead with you—to please, please, PLEASE give this message to any and all brickdicted people you know.

It has been said, "He who has the ability to act, has the responsibility to do so." Now that you have recovered, you have the responsibility to help others do the same.

Here are some ways you can help others:

1. Decide to never, never, NEVER again buy, play with, or even think about, little plastic bricks. Before helping others, you first must

help yourself. So first, be sure you are fully recovered, or at least on the path of recovery.
2. Share this book with any brickdicted AFOLs and others you know. (You could purchase more copies of this book with the money you save by not buying more bricks.) You could do this through your local LUG, or by standing at the entrance to your local toy store, and sharing your story (and this book) with those that come by. Let everyone you come into contact with know that recovery is possible—you're a witness to that. NOTE: Do NOT do this for extended periods of time. The store employees won't like it, and you could get hurt. If you want to go the safer route, you could just go to www.brickdiction.com, and click "Share the Message."
3. Last but not least, you could write a five-star review on Amazon.com. Other potential readers, brickdicted as you once were, will appreciate your review.

I encourage you to spread the message, no matter what stage of recovery you are in. It's just the right thing to do. (Plus it'll allow me to buy more LEGO bricks!)

CONTINUE THE JOURNEY

All of the steps thus far have been steps that need to be done once. This section focuses on continuing the journey, or, in other words, heading in the right direction.

There are two key elements of staying brick-free.

They are:

1. Your Thoughts.

2. Your Actions

It is important that you keep both in check as you continue your recovery.

The First Element – Your Thoughts

You must keep your thoughts in check if you are going to keep away from your brickdiction.

Remember: Any time you start to think about building, constructing, sorting, playing with, modifying, combining, assembling, swooshing, placing, giving, buying, or generally being involved with your bricks, start to think about something else.

Your mind can only hold one thought at a time. So you must replace your brick-ish thoughts with other, healthier ones. When I feel an urge to think about bricks, I think about Mega-blocks. That's all it takes for me, but it might take more for you. Experiment to see what works for you.

The Second Element – Your Actions

The second element you need to succeed, as mentioned before, is your actions. This is just as important, if not even more important than your thinking habits.

Your thoughts lead to your actions, but your actions are where the action happens. (If that makes no sense, don't worry — I don't understand it either).

Don't EVER walk into the toy section of your local, big box store. If you need to buy a gift for a child, let a friend do it for you. Don't EVER pick up a brick. And NEVER go into a room full of MOCs. Doing those things will only push you down.

If you do these two things, you will be on your way to leading a fuller, richer, brick-free life. A life of non-geekiness, free of building and construction. You'll be able to live normally again.

Depending on your situation, you may need to review or even re-do the seven steps from time to time.

You need not be brickdicted. You can be free of plastic bricks forever.

There is hope.

CONFESSION

I have a confession to make.

(Gulp).

I'll confess it quickly, to get it over with as fast as possible:

I'm addicted to LEGO.

If that surprises you, wait until I tell you this:

I don't even mind.

Well, OK, I'm not really *addicted* to LEGO. I just really like it. I kind of love it, actually.

LEGO is amazing. I don't know if you've noticed this, but it has risen in popularity quite a bit over the last few years.

Not very many years ago, if you had picked any random child and asked "What is LEGO?" I think there would have been a fifty-fifty chance the child would be able to answer. Now, LEGO is on the front of every sales leaflet toy companies send out. They're a huge deal. Nowadays, almost any child you asked would be able to tell you not only what LEGO is, but what their favorite set or theme is as well. But it didn't used to be that way.

Which is amazing!

I really don't know why LEGO wasn't more popular years ago. But I do know why they're popular now!

They're popular because of what they provide the builder (whether they're five, fifteen, or fifty).

As I think about LEGO, the number one thing that comes to my mind is creativity. If you're a parent, and you want your child to be creative, then provide them with LEGO—and lots of it! There is no better way to develop creativity than doing some hands-on building.

As a child, I yearned for creative pursuits, and the chance to figure something out on my own. I learned best when using both my hands and my mind.

Think of the skills that LEGO building develops (in both children and adults):

- Creativity.

- Analyzing and decision making. (Which brick should I use? And how? And what color? How can I make this structure stronger?)
- Imagination. (Plotting stories, designing creations, and considering the truly endless possibilities.)
- Following instructions.
- Assembling. (Developing fine motor skills and hand-eye coordination.)
- In group play, social skills and teamwork.
- Self-confidence. (Completing and displaying a model, sharing it with others, and creating something entirely new and original.)

Creativity, particularly, is vital in our day and age. In a world that moves as fast as our world does, future generations need to be able to think creatively, to innovate, to think outside of the box, or to rebuild the box with their LEGO-developed skills.

When a child is stuck on their model, or they don't have the pieces that would make their model complete, they have to think creatively. They have to analyze their options, and then decide between which bricks to use, and how to best use them. This of course will help them in life as they need to make increasingly important decisions.

Of course, they also develop their engineering skills. Allow me to illustrate personally:

When I was quite young, I used to build LEGO walls like this:

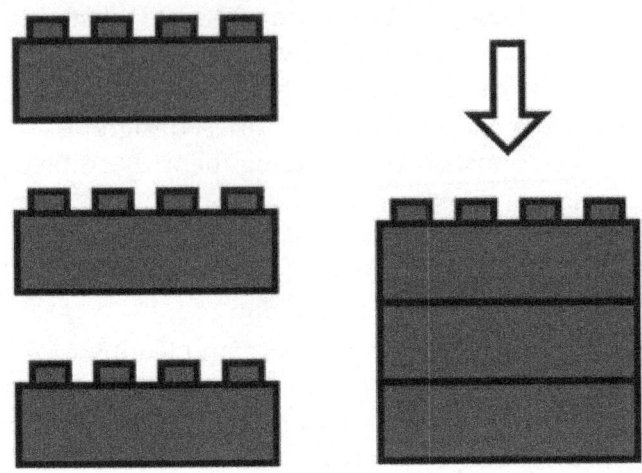

The problem was, the walls were weak. Through hours and hours of play, however, I found a better way to make walls. Using this new method, the walls were incredibly strong:

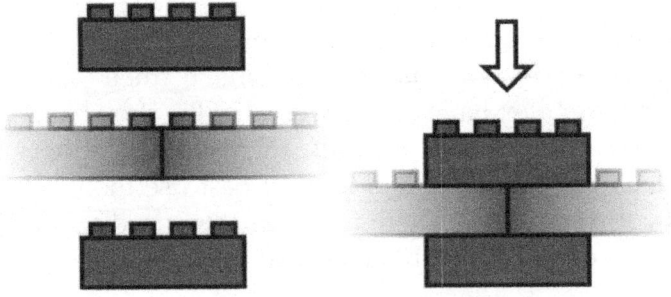

Now, I'm no engineer. It's not something I'd even consider, due to my inner hatred for math. But my point here is not that I would make a bad engineer (I definitely would!) but rather that, through playing with LEGO, I was able to:

1. Try something.
2. Analyze the results (the walls were weak).
3. Realize there was a better way.
4. Decide to use the better way from then on.

I learned to try, I learned to fail, I learned to look for other options, and I learned to move on. All of those, individually, are amazing skills and mindsets to learn. Combined—well, what better skill set could there be?

In a world of gadgets, tools, media, and even toys which dumb us down, and make us mentally stale, LEGO is truly a gem—whatever the builder's age.

Hooray for LEGO!

May you never recover from your brickdiction.

Play well!

THE AUTHOR

ABOUT THE GEEK WHO WROTE THIS BOOK

I think I understand why some adults don't want to play with toys. Maybe they feel childish doing so. Maybe they feel they lose authority, or wisdom, or maturity, or even respect when they act like children. I *think* I understand these people, and the reasons why they don't play like children.

But none of those things really bother me. I'm a proud LEGO fanatic. Yes, I have a child's heart that needs to express itself by playing with tiny plastic people. Yes, I scrimp and save, just to complete my latest MOC. Yes, I…well, you get the point.

That's just who I am — brickdicted.

Writing this "recovery guide" has been a fun experience. It should be noted that I used some ideas from well-known addiction recovery programs (for example, the 12-Step Program). Again, this book is **not** intended to mock serious recovery programs. It *is* meant to mock CFOLs, TFOLs, and AFOLs like me.

Thanks for reading my book. A special thank you to my parents, who created a brick-friendly home environment that developed and encouraged my lifelong brickdiction.

If you want to see some of my MOCs, you can go to www.brickdiction.com.

RESOURCES

Below are a few online resources I've found helpful in fueling my brickdiction.

www.Brickset.com

A great blog for accessing all news related to LEGO. It's also a database of all official LEGO sets past, present, and future. Most sets in the database have reviews including details of that set's playability, overall quality, and value for money. Also a forum.

www.Brothers-Brick.com

Blog featuring exceptional MOCs from many themes, and general LEGO news. Also a resource for reviews and opinions on LEGO products.

www.Eurbobricks.com

"Uniting LEGO fans around the world." Very active forum and blog.

www.FBTB.net

All the news about licensed LEGO themes (especially Star Wars™). Excellent reviews with pictures, and a superb level of detail. Also a forum.

www.TheBrickLife.com

A LEGO blog for families. Written by a mother whose aim is to spread LEGO news and help families make their LEGO hobby affordable.

www.Brickshow.com

Very thorough video reviews of various LEGO sets. Great way to see what LEGO sets look like when being handled and played with.

www.TheBrickBlogger.com

A blog dedicated to those who are discovering or re-discovering the joy and magic of expressing themselves through building with LEGO!

www.Bricklink.com

Think eBay with a LEGO focus. The best place to buy both used and new LEGO bricks.

*We all are blind until we see
That in the human plan
Nothing is worth the making if
It does not make the man.*

*Why build these cities glorious
If man unbuilded goes?
In vain we build the world, unless
The builder also grows.*

Edwin Markham

Made in the USA
Monee, IL
03 May 2026

49437791R00042